Lust and Longing

Mary Metzger

Published by Mary Metzger, 2024.

LUST AND LONGING

First edition. February 24, 2024.

Copyright © 2024 Mary Metzger.

ISBN: 979-8224816651

Written by Mary Metzger.

To E

Lust and Longing

<u>The Longing for Sons</u>

Because all he had ever wanted from life
Was to be his father, be his father's son.
Without a sigh or question,
He took up the earth
That had bent his father's bones
Into its last loamy embrace.
He was sure and thought himself safe.

He married young to a woman younger.
She was beautiful enough to make men envy
And women wonder why him?
The day before Thanksgiving
She gave him his only daughter.
Born without beauty,
She sufficed as a dull addendum
To her mother's life.
She was to him a name he hardly spoke.

Then the sons came.
The first, glorious simply because he was.
As a little boy, he lay in the loft of the barn
Masturbating shafts of dust speckled light.
Later he became entranced by spinning wheels,
And found some happiness in pushing hard against the wind.

The second was pure masculinity lying in his mother's arms.
When he first saw him, he though

"Ah, at last, I have my son."
Years later he would stand close to him in the fields of summer,
Watching the sunset turn small trickles of sweat pink
Against the golden rock of his body,
Feeling profoundly satisfied.
But for it all, the boy winced at the smallest pain,
Rebuked the shortest frustrations by crying out:
"Oh Lord, why me?"
He could only wonder then what kind of man
Would question why he suffered
When suffering was the way of life and the lot of men.
As soon as he could, the boy left for the city.
He came home sometimes.
Gifted his father with soft pastel shirts, silk ties;
His mother with chocolates and hair combs.
He left his father quickly and quietly,
To sit at the woman's side, and talk to her
Long into the night.
His hands fluttered like white flags of surrender
Against the strange and subtle sky.

The last had the beauty of a girl,
And a body slight, but strong as a steel cord.
And as he watched him grow,
Saw in him the love of the land,
He breathed deeply and thought without caution
"Ah, at last, I have my son."

More than anything the boy loved to hunt.
Brought home freshly skinned rabbits,
Offering up their pink and blue flesh
As a bouquet to his mother.

He would butcher defeated deer
Where they lay on the forest floor.
Carry their still-warm flesh home,
His shirt soaked in their blood.
The birds he brought down without respite,
Hanging their corpses like raw rags
Along his mother's clothesline to bleed and age.

He took his surprising wife when he was just seventeen.
An older woman with dark straight hair,
Eyes supple as fine leather, and small breasts.
Just below the surface of her breath, tragedy floated.
She brought with her two young daughters,
Blue-eyed with corn silk hair.
The older, just five, thought herself wise
And knew herself beautiful.
The younger, passed her time
Sucking three fingers while staring solemnly at the sky.
She seldom spoke and, as time passed, became mute.

His father was all the prouder then.
"It is a real man who raises children that are not his spawn."
His pride became boundless when he became a grandfather.
Again, and then again and yet again, in quick succession,
His handsome grandsons came.

In evenings, in the summer,
He lay in his bed and heard,
Coming from across the pasture,
From the home he had built for his son and his family,
The boy's wife screaming and begging,

The girls crying out in their night
And nothing else.

In the morning, when it was time to work,
His last son smiled and said, "Hi Pop."
He looked into his eyes,
Saw down beneath his long lashes,
A secret evil, a great corruption.
He felt his bones become wind chimes
Dusted with frost,
Hanging in a tree above his father's grave.

A Daughters Longing

We were not the children
Conceived in their minds,
Nor for us the secret rituals of their nights,
It was not of us they dreamed,
We were born dull with their pain,
Dry with their disappointment.

They muted us with their milk,
We turned to stones in their arms,
Heavy burdens to be carried.
Like small, stunned calves
We struggled to stand alone.

Our love weaned from bitterness
We sat at their tables
Heads bowed
Eating morsels of jealousy,

Consuming slices of solitude.

Small sepia portraits lost to fear.
Silence the beginning of our pain
Silence marking its end.
We hugged ourselves close in the night
Asking "Mother, can you feel me?"

Their indifference a wound
Bandaged in thin victories
We learned the limits of our fires
Where their coldness began.
Our mirrors shattered
Before the hardness of their words.

We filled our bags with sharp shards of shame,
Tiny brittle unenvied crusts of bread,
Buttons from their coats
Dried roses from their bouquets.
Clinging to them as we were going.
Asking "Mother will you think of me?"

We would pour our thick grief
Into the arms of their apparitions
Putting pain in the envelope of lust
Sealing it with slick tongues
Fingers weary and wet
Asking "When will I be enough?"

Thirteen Ways of Looking at a Longed-for Woman

After Wallace Stevens Thirteen Ways of Looking at a Blackbird

1.

In the enchantment of self-conscious simile
in that enchanted enclave of four
I first saw myself a she-wolf searching nimbly
for the sacramental scent of her.

2.

In the enchantment of self-conscious simile,
I entered through an enigmatic door.
A simple blackbird in simple blackness
Still searching for the complex light of her.

3.

I was of three minds then,
not one of them quite set
one longing, one longed for,
the other longing yet.

4.

She spoke to me as if I were her child:
"Come whisper in my ear."
Not knowing that I was a she-wolf
With a fear of coming near.

5.

I sat upon the highest chair
Small seeds and crumbs to eat,
Then went and nestled in her hair,
Then danced upon my feet.

6.

I spoke to her of a she-wolf's desire
For a new mountain to climb,
Feeling the phantom of our desire
Clarifying over time.

7.

I know all a blackbird knows
So, know the song she sings,
The joy of innuendos,
Her voice beneath my wings.

8.

I see all a blackbird sees
With eyes small and smart and swift,
From the tops of lusting trees,

I looked down upon her gift.

9.

I know all a wild wolf knows
Of songs and how to sing,
Sense in the shiver of the snows
The warmth her blood could bring.

10.

I see what a she-wolf sees
When her eyes come narrow and clear,
Feel myself unable to flee
When I hold her reflection here?

11.

Not knowing the ways of wild things,
She moved too quick to bring us near,
So made the blackbird stretch out its wings
The she-wolf back away in fear.

12.

The blackbird taken by her charm
Tried again to leave her nest.
Making her wing into an arm
She reached out for her breast.

13.

When she came to ask us why
O if perhaps we were afraid
We held our heads low and shy,
Before the truth of what she said.

Alliterations of "S "in Impact Font

A shallow summer
devoid of sweltering sun, deep heat.
simple and serene
sets the stage for the
spinning out of alliterations.

To swaddle you in S:
start by speaking
the slenderness of your shoulders,
how shyness sways your silhouette,
sends your shadow sideways.

How for all its softness
Sometimes I swear I can swim.
in the sureness of your sound

You smile is a secure secret,
and when you smile at me,
I seem a second secret
set to surface.

Spreading a shore of similes,

I want, and want to say in S:

the smell of shells.
the sense of soft swollen stones
slippery and slick.
shuddering waves,
something of
soundlessness and satisfaction.

Of sound and satisfaction,
and salt and saliva.
of somewhere and
something else
somehow.

<u>The Longing Embrace</u>

A slight embrace,
And I read our book:
Tree set like stone,
Root roads,
Branches winding like rivers,
But set and set.

You the unsettling wind,
Moving through me,
Denying the reality of my atoms
Raising whispers from my leaves,
Evoking the longing for wings.

The Longing for Your Sound

Of all your secrets, which is most profound
Is hidden neither in your heart or mind,
But in the silence that protects your sound.
You are hidden, impossible to find.

The words themselves easy enough to say,
But it is your sound amid the clatter
That will at last give your secrets away,
For it alone tells what the matter is.

It takes so much effort to tell the lie,
Far easier to speak the truthful taunt,
Than to listen to them when they bleed and cry,
"I will speak to you when and if I want."

And then what is it their ears can do,
But wait attentive for the sound of you?

Longing for Contrition

Saying I will love her not, never again, not at all
So, I promised myself at the beginning of fall,
Later I gathered the petals of dried morning glory,
Said, as I threw them, crisp and beige, off the balcony
Their purple has faded, their glorious mornings gone
My love for you will lose its color; I will move on.

When in their mourning for the sun the trees turned yellow,
I thought of you not but dreamed of you on my pillow.

In the black of night becoming what impossible seems,
An old woman dreaming a young woman's dreams.
I knew then that my will went so far and no further.
Though I thought of you not, I could dream of no other.

In the cold I heard the leaves crash with a thud to earth,
I desired a Siren to lure away my breath,
When in the white, in the gray I found I could not bury,
Rituals of our motions branded in memory.
Even as I walked Moscow's streets sheened is thick, slick ice,
I understood well my foolish, my sad sacrifice.
Riding my high horse, nostrils flared in indignation.
What victory was won but my own desperation?

By spring my pride was broken on longing's painful rack,
And I wanted nothing more than you're taking me back.
Without searching I found you where, as I knew you would be
Practicing rituals in the square where all could see.
At the statue to Mourning Mothers I bent my knee,
Prayed "I am sorry for having offended thee."
How I detest my ego, my righteous, my pride,
As if anything mattered more than you by my side.

Algebra for Longing

Some soundless sound
Woke me from my deep sleep,
And I rose, went to my table
Caught your poised words
Just as they arrived.

Their rhythm not a poet's rhythm,
But a mathematician's, written
Out like an algebraic equation:
Ten words and then the break,
Then five and then a pause,
And then the next five, and
Then the symbolic conclusion.

They are monosyllabic, minimalist,
Saying only what is needed,
A fine sparse reduction concluding
In a formula for affection.

I will not lie. I would have, as I
Always do, wished for more. For
Your love written out, for the
Obligation to be erased by desire.
Yet, still, it was you who wrote.
I carried your words back
Under the blankets with me,
Pretending you were sleeping next to me,
Our feet woven together like lovers'.
I slept once again.

Longing for An Old Woman's Regret

Never having understood love.
Thinking that it was a fish to be caught,
A fast ball moving toward the catcher's glove.
As if the wind blew in one direction only.

A Young Woman's Question; An Old Woman's Answer

"If LOVE is from God,
Why are we so bad at receiving it?
If Love is a gift so precious,
Then why should it hurt like a wound?
If lOve completes us like mothers milk, and fathers grave
Why should it freeze us like ice, or burn like a brand?
If loVe is about two becoming one,
Why should we not look for the piece that fits?
If lovE always ends,
why not choose the best?"

The Old Woman's Answer:

Oh, the secure presumptions of the sure,
The young, the safe, the religious, the pure.
Who stumble on one truth, one thing, one way,
Cling to its safety until their last day.

I do envy them their absolute truth,
That requires neither testing nor proof,
Perhaps just the Bible, or one great book
And then there is only that one place to look.

Theirs is the logic of Aristotle
Or of Zeno with his famous turtle,
That sees things as one way or the other,
Not the either and or bound together.

The logic that claims change is illusion
To think otherwise but a delusion.
But I, the student of Hegel's great mind,
Practice the logic of another kind.

It sees things not in terms of either /or
But as both and yet something else and more.
Have not all the great poets said as much:
To be wary of fate's deceitful touch.

So that just as we think we are the best,
And so, stand over and above the rest,
Things change, and we fall from our glory
Caesar, Bonaparte, Czar say that story.

What is best today, is gone tomorrow
Bitter bile is the taste of that sorrow,
Better understand what the Buddha knew,
That we are just a passing, passing through.

True human beings with their frail, fragile hearts
Also have other, stronger, more solid parts,
So that love is suffering and glory,
A truly triumphant and tragic story.

And that those we love, we love as they are
Not as some wish we make upon a star,
In spite, not because of imperfections
The heart, not the mind, makes our connections.

Elizabeth Bishop's *The Fish*

I am the fish of her poem now,
I wake in the mornings, my gills
Weary from their nocturnal struggle
Against the air. Pale brown rosettes
Lie flat against my skin

There are no white sea lice to eat at me,
But my flesh has lost its tension ,
Hangs like those green weeds from my body.
Inside, my bones are eroding, and like that
Coarse white flesh, they are packed painfully
Hard together.

My eyes are tin foiled from within by shiny flakes,
Strange, translucent creatures float across
their clear water. I watch the world always
Through old, scratched isinglass.
I am blind and getting blinder.

In my weary lip I hold many hooks, each
A reminder of some great battle fought
And won against some enemy destined to
Feed off of me. Nothing has changed.

Old fish, old woman, old poet, old lover
Having survived, let go now without a struggle,
Into the jubilant rainbow water.

The Calla Lily Ghost

A Calla Lily,
Is a Calla
Is a Lily

Is a man,
Is a woman,
Is a ghost

Is a ghost haunting
Is a woman taunting
Her lovers' wanting

Is a ghost walking
Is a woman stumbling
Along Kuznetsky Most,

Is a haunting, taunting
Ghostly lily woman shredding
The streets of Moscow

Casting Light

The sun slices Moscow open
And everything has changed.
The black branches of yesterday

Were gilded silver during the night

The leaves so still and gray
Are today tinted with pink,
They dance a jig to the wind's fiddle.
Here and there, one is still able to see,
Within the pale carpet of winter grass,
Small strands of green floss

I will see you today. Then
This day will become
A hot loaf of bread,
Dripping with butter.

Moscow Lover

In a wintered spring that refuses to unbutton itself,
In a city of golden domes where Others sit
And conserve what needs to be destroyed,
In a park where your body
Glides among the other birds,
I am a stiff stick
Longing for your supple wing
To cover me.

Then there is you, and then there is me.
I am no fool to deny inclinations,
Nor so blind as to need eyes to see,
My touch knows the allowance you give it,
In this city that does not allow us to be.

If it were enough that our touches
Could speak our caring,
Or the coded messages of our gazes,
Could say all that needed to be said.
If nothing needed to be hidden,
Perhaps for better, perhaps for worse,
things would be different,
Yet still as certain.

The language is a hard wall to pass over.
I speak and you do not understand me,
You speak and I feel myself sink into
Dark waters of incomprehensibility.
I fear I can never tell you my secrets,
I fear I can never learn yours.
What are women without their words?

And so, it is all these things,
That under the pull of our gravity
Take the form of a single sphere,
Rolling this way and that, yet,
Unable to gather the momentum
To disappear over the rims and edges
Of your certain almond eyes,

Amongst prohibitions; all these things
That are fearful and strange and difficult,
Through separations and fluctuations,
The silence that evolves from spoken words,
All that seems insurmountable,
In this city,
I am certain.

<u>Confession</u>

As I was leaving, I slipped it into my pocket
A piece of the sweetness you surrounded yourself with
Yet never consumed.
I stole it without contrition; that thing that revealed you:
A woman who kept temptation close to feed off its denial.

In the taking it was transformed.
No longer a small piece of chocolate,
It became a repository of your essence,
A thing once yours and now mine.
Something sacred I took home and offered up
To the small green Buddha, I sat before.

Lest my confession be incomplete
I should tell you that I fantasized
Sucking away its layers,
Sending my tongue to search for its center,
Letting its sweetness gather
In the crevices of my mouth.
I would not have, as you did,
Denied myself that particular pleasure.

In the morning, to save it from the sun,
I moved it into the slim shadow of curled bamboo
Growing in a bottle that looked like a lighthouse.
It had once held wine flavored with the bitter taste of cranberry
That I drank one night to soften my longing for you,
Before I wandered down to the club
To dance myself into exhaustion

Until a woman with black eyes
Looked at me too hard and too long
And I left with her.

In the evening, fearful of what the cats might do
I moved it onto the small table in the living room,
Near the picture of my daughters and me
On the deck of the house, I had rented in the Poconos
In July of the year, I had broken up with my lover.
On the first night I cried for her and was ashamed for it.
The next afternoon we found a small snake
A ribbon hidden in the rocks
Along the stream where we had gone to wade.

The chocolate was still on the table the next afternoon,
When my grandson came to visit.
He asked me for it with his eyes.
Unwrapping its gold foil, I handed it to him
Stood listening to his soft sounds of pleasure
As he ate it.

Warrior in a Murmuration of Snowflakes

It was not a confused snow
Large flakes bobbing and drifting on meek drafts,
Uncertain where to land.

Nor was it a helpless snow,
Each flake driven to its end
By a commanding wind.

Neither was it a diamond crystal snow,
Each particulate sparkling in the light,
As, shot by a cruel wind,
it sandblasted the skin

It was instead a mystical murmuration
Of imperceptible flakes
undulating this way and that.
a gray veil floating on calm currents,
willfully defying descent.
I recognized it for what it was:
A beckoning.

It was in that snow on that night,
In Afghan Park, in Moscow, in Russia
That we stood -
Our swords close to our bodies,
Tips resting lightly on our shoulders,
Our eyes fixed on her,
Waiting for our lesson to begin.

Within the undulating veil she began to move:
bent her knees, tilted her sword so that it lay across her arm.
No longer a sword, it became a mirror
In which she saw the unseen.
Her right hand lifted to grasp the handle,
And the sword swung behind her,
Then over her shoulder
Before she brought it down, swift, and hard.
Slicing an opening into another dimension.
There her essence appeared:
Pure warrior spirit moving in eternal murmuration.

<u>Tides</u>

Your tide risen to the watermark of comfort.
You float, mute and disconnected.
An abandoned ship on surreal waters.

For my part it is no matter,
The sea neither churns nor gently rocks.
My old boat glides on perfectly placid waters.

Yet you should know that the words
With the anticipation of the unconceived,
Of the created before creation,
Churn and roil against the rocks,
Restless and restless.

They do not understand
why you will not give me
A poem to write.
Or speak the words that will
Allow me to speak the words.

Heavy with their own weightlessness,
They are, after all, yet not.

<u>What Can I Say?</u>

What can I say my beloved?
You are not what I wanted,
Nor what I need. You are not some

dream fulfilled. Our relationship
Is wrought with its tragedies and pains.
You leave me longing, always wanting.
Continents separate us, and you,
With your withdrawals, and I with
My thin blood, what do we do?
But I know, that no matter what
Or perhaps because of it all,
You are the great love of my long life.

<u>What If?</u>

What would it have been like
If instead of meeting you in
Some sad and seedy women's bar,
Introduced to each other by your lover,
I had met you quite casually
At the supermarket, our fingers touching
As we reached for the same piece of fruit?

Would the sight of your fingers still have aroused me?
Would you have felt the rise of my desire?
Would you have spoken to me
Or turned your head away and
Forced me to speak to you first?

What would have happened,
If your breasts had accidentally
Brushed against mine as we
Passed through the same door:
Would I have trembled, lifted my
Head to look at you? Would you

Have felt me tremble, would you
Have known?

Or if it was tomorrow, on the
Streets of Moscow, and I saw
Your bowed head as we walked
Across the alley. Would you
Have felt my eyes? Would you
Have met mine? Would either
O us have known what we wanted?

And if it was to be, would we,
Strangers, simply have gone
With each other somewhere,
Simply to fuck...simply that?

Would I have kissed you as deeply,
And not had to turn away?
Would we have been free of
Our shyness, our inhibitions?

And if I asked you to, would
You have bound me to the bed,
And if you asked me, would I
Have let you bleed my passion?
When I begged you to stop, would you have?
When I asked you for more,
Would you have taken me to another level?

Would you have let me bring you
Into my mouth, suckle your clit?

Would you have let me draw back
The hood with my fingers, flick
Its tip with my tongue?
Would you have let me
Find the secrets places deep inside you?
Would you have?
Would you have made me scream
As I came; could I have made you?

And when it was over, would we
Have showered together, had sex
there one last time, and then dressed,
hugged, walked away from one another?
Would it have been better?

<u>When Mathematicians Go Insane - Written for my longed-for mathematician.</u>

When mathematicians go insane
They become poets,
Although they never realize it,
Their insanity being just that.

It begins with a subtle aura of fatality,
Giving way to subdued surely
That the proud brilliance of their youth,
Has begun its inevitable diminution.,

It accelerates in amphetamine fueled
Champers of denial in which,
Caught up in the intense rush of becoming,

They bite small pieces of dead flesh
From that which is still living.

Sometime later,
The exquisite physical beauty of pi
Traces across their minds,
And afterwards, they begin to compute
The regression of cold February nights,
The infinity of snowflakes.
Rapturous, they ascend into the ether of abstraction
Where they encounter the ontological passion of words.
How they yearn and lust for one another,
How in their longing, they call out for others?
How they entwine and interpenetrate
Bringing into being kaleidoscopic totalities.
At an even higher level of abstraction
The transformative power of words
Appears before their consciousness
And they come to know
The profound significance of simile
And Metaphor leaves them amazed.

At the highest level of abstraction,
Stripped of power and meaning
Words stand naked before them
Exposing themselves as pure sound.

Afterwards they can be found,
Sitting at their desks
Tapping out the rhythm of iambic pentameter or,
Perhaps wandering some campus path,
Repeating over and over again,

"Attenuated, attenuated"
Enthralled by the sound.

The transformation complete,
They write great dada poetry
Perhaps something in the style of Tzara:
"Mean, Median, Mode, Moan
Approximate woman standing alone
Isolation's standard deviation,
Squared soft separation."

The sadness of it being
That they think they are writing mathematical proofs.
In their more lucid moments, they realize they are not
And grabbing their heads they cry out:
"I have lost my mind. I have lost my mind.

Wind

The drawn-out pitch of a tin flute
Pulls me half-awake from a sleep
That will be slept in phases
And without dreams.
No matter, I dreamed with you before I slept
Laying bare the wounds inflicted
By the extremes of my love for you.

A few hours later, the wind whistles like
A small child just mastering the balance
Between breath and lips, and I turn beneath
The deep layers of down,

Ponderous, pondering

Just before dawn, I am awakened by
The familiar sound of a train whistle and know
It for what it is, the Susquehanna line running
Through Scranton, through Wilkes Barre,
Down into the valley to pick up a load of coal.

And I remembered how I dreamt last night,
Before I laid down to sleep, of walking the rails:
My hand a child's hand, gathered up in yours.

In the light, the noise of the wind is irritating,
It takes the sound of water, become steam,
Become pressure releasing through the
tiny valve of a tea kettle. It shrieks.

I open my eyes and watch the larger birds,
Taking off like jets into the gray sky,
Then shut them again.

I remembered that before I slept
I dreamt I was reading our love.

I stand before the window with my coffee and see
That the wind has driven the trees insane.
A great psychotic birch lurches at me and then recedes.
Smaller ones daven before the wind's wailing wall,
And the smallest, fevered, and frenzied,
Rock back and forth, heel to toe, heel to toe,
Their leaves flapping against the air.

I my dream with you last night,
driven half insane by love
I rocked from side to side as I cried.

In Time

There was a time I took
Whatever you offered:

Never Calla Lily bouquets in tender
Paper, nor boxes containing hearts
Of Venetian glass,
But kisses, given through closed lips.
Chocolates wrapped in golden foil.
Pistachios and peanuts
That rimmed the mouth
With salt.

Small lemon tartlets in cardboard boxes,
Snippets of news,
Stand as remanent of
Your sequestered time.

And always dinners:
Dinners during which you
Never seemed to tire of
Eating redundancies,
Nor I of listening to them:

Of sushi, sashimi
In plastic boxes with black bottoms,

Pizza delivered in gray cardboard,
Packets of smoked fish,
Containers of sodden
Salads, tins of caviar, rimed cheeses,
Roasted red shells of lobster
Eaten from your table.
And the bottles too:
Of Italian wine, Kentucky bourbon,
French champagne sipped from Baccarat
But not yet of fine Russian vodka.

Dinners that never were,
When I went to sleep hungry.

Dinners after which
You reminded me
To take out the garbage,
When I left in the morning.
"Before ten please."
And I took it.

Contradictions

You are a woman of images
And I, a woman of words;
You are a long and slender string,
And I the hollow along which it is tightened.
You are the button,
And I a space for you to pass through;
You constantly ponder the future,
I, am the pondered past;
You, are the inexplicable,

I, the explicator.

We are two different trees growing in the same forest.
To different forests growing the same tree;
Our branches bending towards one another

<u>Immortality</u>

Before the Russian winter, I feel myself become Zhivago,
And you, my Lara, sleeping somewhere in the distance.
It is I who trek across the endless snow,
Step by step engraving it with my need.

It is my heart, made thin and weary
From the unremitting longing,
Scarred by silence,
Which refuses to believe it is not you
I see in the street.

It is I and not he, who stands alone before the window,
Etching your name into frozen crystal, waiting for the poem
That will make you immortal.

<u>Continued Conversations with Gertrude</u>

"Another button, another bowl?"
She is a parrot
Perched on mockery.

I pretend not to be apprehended.
"But Gertie, she goes straight.

Directly to the eye."

"Hmmm she presents
Hmmmm, a little longer"
"Is she like a quilt or a flower?"
She tomes.

"More isinglass with a hint
Of bergamot

She smiles, tilts her head back,
Runs one hand through
Her short hair, and pauses
To adjust her breath before:

"Oh, so grand for you in
the moment you know now, and
feeling all home free all."

"I thought you would notice that"
I answer.
"And your advice?"

"Shared semiotics."
and sits still.

Then, stopping to adjust her vest
off she goes.

<u>Last Poem</u>

On wings of bone and feathers,
Bones of balsam, feathers of twill,
On the drafts of supplications
I glide, neither rising nor falling.

Unsure whether I am falcon or wren,
Uncertain as to where or when
I should land; knowing the time is never right,

Your neck slackens, your head bends
And you are asleep.
In the night, your hair blooms,
Your sockets bleed black.
My wings, Spanish fans stroke the air
To the temple of your breath, are tireless
I circle the periphery of your limits,
Filled with desire.

<u>Do You Remember?</u>

When the trees were warriors

And the wind was their strength?
How brutal their branches,
How swift their blows?

How bravely they fought
On the pure blue field of battle?

And the patient earth,
How it waited for their leaves?
And when they fell, how gently they went
To their rest?

I wondered if you understood then
How bravely I fought without the wind
Throughout the seasons of you suspicion,
Against the enemy of you distrust.
My battlefield how it trembled.
How, because you, you were the prize,
I never rested, never fell.

Zhivago's Woman

I sit, a sentinel without sight
Witness to the moon's horrific light.
A landscape rendering gray on grey
Camouflaging them to hunt their prey.

She is a study in black and white
Sleek obsidian, warmed anthracite
Cast against the white marble's luminous glow
She sleeps, woman painted chiaroscuro.
I pass a palm across extremes,
Pray poetry into her dreams.

Leave love clarified in black and white
Enter their monochromatic night.
Hear the alpha male's conscious breath
His focused meditation on death,

Anticipation breaking silver crust
Moaning in the anguish of the blood lust.

They smell me, a woman standing on the stairs,
In the matte night feel the advantage theirs.
But I am a poet; know well the power of the word
Even blinded by monotony, I will still be heard.

I clap my hands, hear my voice echo "No."
Feel fear flee across malevolent snow.

While firelight dances on ebony hair
I return once again to my poet's chair.
Pick up my pen and begin to write
My love for her in black and white.

<u>Uneclipsed</u>

Do you think I would mourn your moon
Because it had eclipsed?
Because I could not see you,
You had lost your power to move my tide?
Because I could not hear you,
That I would no longer sing you my song?
Did you think because I could no longer touch you,
My fingers could no longer trace you image,
Or because you were not with me,
That you were without me!

Do you think my love is the frail bone of a bird
That would be broken by the bold wind of you eclipse;

A mirror, that would shatter without you reflection?

As if your dam could hold in check
The power of my longing?
As if my love was not itself a force.

<u>You</u>

You were my beloved,
Long, long
Before your eyes held my reflection.

When I laid
Watching frozen crystals
Dripping fantasy
Outside my window,
You were already my desire.

In the simple movement
Of my arms sliding across paper,
A soft scratch in a stillness so sharp,
It summoned sound from the snow,
As it surrendered to the night,
I loved you and recalled my love.
Embraced you with my words,
I wrote my yearning for you.

When my small ambition of azaleas
Bloomed multicolored
Yellow, orange, deeper orange, yet
Purled against white

Laying against one another,
Then too, you were loved.

When I knelt down on well worked soil
Brough my head close to the earth
So that I breathed in the ancient smell,
Pressed my fingers into it
And felt is soft yielding,
I cherished you.

When I stood still and silent
In the morning mist,
Licking my lips, tasting salt,
Feeling an unseen mouth,
Tug quick and urgent on my line,
Twitching back my arm in response,
I knew my love for you in that moment.

You were mine, my beloved,
When the smell of honeysuckle
Left me sleepless
So that I went to my garden,
To the fence where it hung,
And stood there
White in the moonlight,
Sucking sweet nectar,
Dreaming of you.

When I walked through fall forests
The dog dancing at my feet
Sleek and solid, stirring the leaves,
The loping off

I saw my breath
Felt the softness I carried with me for you.

Even when I lost myself in another woman's body
Yet, still, you were my beloved,
My one desire.
Across seasons and rooms
I watched you,
Wanted you,
Waited for you.

I loved you for long, long
Before I first heard the sound of your voice,
Before I shook you hand,
Before we moved with each other to throbbing music,
Before you kissed me on the cheek
Before I you felt me, before I felt you,
Before you and I bathed each other
You hand soapy silk on my breast
Before we made each other moan
Before I fell asleep with the taste of you
Before you awoke,
Before you laid your shorn head
Soft and slow, next to mine,
Told me you loved me,
Asked me if I loved you,
I did.

The Lioness

Entering the same dark cave,
Like two stealthy lionesses

Approaching each other
On a sultry, savannah night,
We sense rather than see the other,
Begin our ritualistic stalking.

We move in and out of deep darkness
Dodging the colored spears of light
That threaten to expose us,
Reveal our search.

We pursue each other through
The thick, oily matching made mist.
All cat cool, calm and casual.
Self-contained.

Yet there is something in the set of our eyes,
The slackness of our jaws,
The quick moving in and out of our chests,
That lays naked our vulnerability to each other
All the lust and whatever is left of love.

That night,
We were caught by the same blue star light
At the same moment.
We lifted our heads
From beneath our hunched soldiers
Met eye to eye.
And the only familiar softness fell on us
Like tiny, dry red leaves
We stood motionless,
Embracing with our eyes.
Held each other

For so long and so short a time,
Let go reluctantly
We turned our heads
And the darkness came once again.

I wanted to lean my body against you,
To take your face in my hands,
Touch my head to yours,
Whisper the mantra of desire.

Instead, I took my woman by the hand
Led her to the dance floor,
A few moments later,
You did the same,
And we dance,
Arching with the acuteness of our awareness.

Harem

Set stark against pure polarity
She bleeds a man's need
For the endless accumulation of women.
She is a woman subtly, nearly imperceptibly
Building her harem.

Sometimes she assumes the guise of a giant condor
Gliding slowly towards them from
Inconceivable heights: she blocks the light
And while they are confused by the darkness
She gathers them one by one into her.

To some she shows her essence:
A peacock resplendent in his display
Knowing that they will supplicate
Before his haughty show.

For those who would have it otherwise,
She appears,
A woman of shy, self-conscious, beauty,
Her head tilting or bowed, her eyes demure.

They envision her then as a tree that must be climbed
An exotic perfume that must be worn,
Thick Italian wine that must be poured into their glasses.
And so
In their desire to possess her, they become her possessions

To those whose hearts are vulnerable,
She exposes herself, a violated swan,
Neither black nor white, but gray
Carrying her suffering across the turbid waters of the moon.
As they are drawn closer
She asks them to become thinner,
And they become thinner,
She asks them to become lighter,
And they become lighter yet,
Until they follow weightless in her wake.

In the darkness she imprints herself upon them
Offers them what is too much for them to bear
She moves from one to the other,
Her arms filling with each new vision
Her vision filling each new pair of arms.

Not understanding
That the end was written into the beginning,
Some stand in doorways reluctant to leave
When their appointed time is done.
These she excises with the scalpel of her rage.
Banished from the harem, they return often
To claw at its entrance until they bleed.
They are forgiven and taken back
But not before they have sworn submission.

The obedient she gathers round her table;
Feeds them salted pleasures and pungent delights,
Waters their gardens with champagne
Dusts their ears with attention.

They play poker, bidding up the pot.
Some understanding the rules of the game
The others not.

<u>For Olga</u>

What can I possibly say

To one so young,

She glides on sheer friction
Across the flawless skin

Of ice

Can I tell her that

She barely touches the earth as she
Runs across summer and winter,
Heedless of the grass she punishes,
Forgetful of her imprints in the snow.

She thinks she believes nothing is impossible,
But she believes differently.

When she thinks of love,
She thinks of things tempered
And tame and untarnished,
Not of its explosive fury
Which is at once passion and pulse,
Nor of what is wild in it, nor its blemishes.

I know that to love someone impossible,
Imperfect, without regret is what love is.
To endure all without complaining
Without turning away, that, too, is love.

But she recoils before pain as if
That was the thing to do; she licks
Her wounds before they have finished bleeding,
And then turns away as if rejection
Were the end and not the beginning of love;
As if it really mattered.

How can I tell her that
The earth is my beloved now,

She, who across the years
Has gifted me,
With exquisite perfumes,
With bountiful bouquets of flowers,
Sweet fruits and tender caresses.
Who or what have I loved more?

We have courted each other long,
And I wait for her to at last
To Open herself and take me in,
Leaving behind the young
To make their impressions.
But it was not to be.

Homeless Beneath the Moon

Into the night he releases
His wordless poem,
Rhythmic and perfectly metered.
Then pauses to consider it
Before a new trope of sound
Rises with the steam from his mouth.

This cold winter, this Moscow night,
Loneliness, or some ancient ache
For belonging is our common inspiration.
But I am the lesser poet,
In need of words to beg beneath the moon.

<u>Fractal of Faith</u>

I must believe
That our reiterations:
Intimacy to distance
Chaos to order,
kindness to cruelty,
Produce a pattern
So complex and beautiful,
It rises to the level of infinity.

Not to do so would mean
That I could no longer weave
Words into one another,
Nor knead the dough
That will become the bread
That feeds us:
I, the poet who needs to love,
You, the need to be loved.

<u>And What About Me?</u>

The cold of ancient times
The cold of distant places,
Blows inland from the Baltic
And everything is brittle,
Everything is dry.

And everything is so fragile
As I sit to write,
Calling up the memory

Of a scene acted out
Before a fireplace, in a play
She had written for us.

How warm it was, the flames
Dancing orange callas,
The feeling of her there next
To me, the expensive wine
Braising my chest.
How soft, how warm her voice
When she branded my heart
"And what about me?"

How long ago was that now the poet wonders,
A day, a month, a year ago?
Certainly, it was after she had left
Her beloved, and before she had returned to
those comforting arms.

Everything is dry and brittle and
so very fragile as I begin my poem

<u>Suddenly Winter</u>

It is the very beginning of summer
And the grass is not yet sweet, not yet fattened.
It will be some time before it is brazed
By the August sun
And winter is unremembered, and I'll conceived
The earth is just warm enough to be fragrant,
And just fragrant enough to make your fingers dream.

You cannot see her, but you sense her,
Waiting there; a mystery on the other side of the
Summer meadow,
And you, standing on the very edge,
Are moved at last by the need for a solution.
Perfect Fibonacci sequences suffer
Beneath the weight of your journey,
Their cries of course, go unheard.
Blind to omens, you irresistibly move on.

You first see her as from a great distance,
Unclear, undefined.
And nothing will seem more important to you,
Than coming closer.
You quicken, imagining yourself
A sleek and supple girl.
Running through clouds of dandelions.
You cannot stop and it is impossible
To think of a time before.

When you at last come as close
As knife to bone,
You see that her eyes are made of gold and jade,
That her lips blush and in her hair,
Secrets, written as mathematical equations,
Are woven.
Red rivers run beneath her skin and flow
To the very tips of her blood red fingernails.
The fact that duplicity melts
The corners of her mouth,
Does not dissuade you, and when
She lowers her head shyly,

Then raises it again to confront you
With her questions,
You will feel ashamed
And apologize for who you are.

When you first hear her voice,
She will not be talking to you.
But to one of her other lovers,
And though you are standing on stone,
The taste of sweetgrass will fill
The crevices of your mouth,
Your temples will throb to the beat
Of her cadence,
And you will become a poet,
Writing in keeping with her rhythm.
Time will have only two dimensions then:
Before her and after her.

With her arrows, she will shoot sorrow at you,
And you will wonder how she could have
Given you so much pain to bear without wounds.
Much later you will notice how easily she bleeds,
Because you are a woman,
You will love her more,
And set your clock
To the tempo of her needs.

When she denies you, you will say,
"Ah, I never wanted your body or time.
I never really wanted to see the sun
When it kissed your throat,
Or know what you dreamed

In the slices of your night"
The fact that you have never heard
Her heartbeat,
Will seem absolutely inconsequential for a time,
And you will feed on moments
That come fitfully. You will eat
Small dry crumbs of black bread
And declare yourself full.

One day you will walk from her door,
And it will be winter,
And you will notice that the grass
Is no longer sweet, that it is now shrill
And lays at your feet broken.
Fathered by a distant demented river.
You will feel your fingers grow numb,
And then your desire, and at last your heart
As you walk across the street.

<u>The Fury of Champagne – After Pablo Neruda</u>

I LOVE YOU AS COMPLEX AND MYSTERIOUS THINGS
ARE MEANT TO BE LOVED.

I LOVED YOU WHEN I DID NOT KNOW IT
I LOVED YOU WITHOUT SEEING YOU
I LOVED YOU WITHOUT KNOWING HOW TO.
I LOVED YOU KNOWING ITS FUTILITY
I LOVED YOU SECRETLY, IN THE DARKNESS THAT
BELONGED TO ME.
I LOVED YOU TRANSPARENTLY WHEN YOU NEEDED ME
TO.

I LOVED YOU BECAUSE YOUR DREAMS WERE INDUCED
I LOVED YOU BECAUSE WHEN YOU SLEPT YOU WERE
UNSURE OF THE DAY OR THE NIGHT
BECAUSE WHEN YOU AWOKE, YOU STRUCTURED THE
SILENCE WITH YOUR SOUND
BECAUSE YOUR BRILLIANCE SLIT THE WORLD OPEN
AND ITS COLORS FELL AT MY FEET.
BECAUSE YOUR HEART PUNCTURED THE SKY AND IT
BLED BLUE INTO MY EYES.

I LOVE YOU BECAUSE OF ALL POSSIBLE TRUTHS IT IS
YOURS THAT FILLS ME
BECAUSE OF ALL POSSIBLE LIES IT IS YOURS THAT
PERSUADES ME
BECAUSE WHEN I WAS LOST YOU FOUND ME
BECAUSE WHEN YOU FOUND ME, I WAS LOST IN YOU
BECAUSE WHEN YOU SPEAK, I HEAR WHAT YOU DO NOT
SAY
BECAUSE YOUR FEET ARE MY ROOTS
BECAUSE YOUR FINGERS LEAVE POEMS WHEREVER THEY
TOUCH ME
BECAUSE YOUR EYES JUDGE AND BECAUSE THEY
FORGIVE
BECAUSE THEY HOLD ME AS IF THEY WERE ARMS
BECAUSE YOU ARE THE FURY OF CHAMPAGNE
TRAPPED BY A CORK
IN A BOTTLE I AM AFRAID TO OPEN.

<u>Before</u>

Before I was ten,
I knew myself for what I was, absolutely alone.
I awoke alone, one morning, alone,
The season was a summer of solitude,
While a sea breeze swayed the curtains,
And the heated light took me up,
I lifted my head from my solitary pillow,
Saw, at the foot of the bed,
The spirit of my guardian angel,
Alone with me.

Another time I was sleeping in
An empty house, and I awoke
To find my grandmother in the
Rocking chair in the corner. She
Rocked and spoke to me for
Hours, and I, so eased by
Her presence, slept the secure sleep
Of the child that does not sleep alone.
In the morning she was gone, and
I was alone again in an empty
House by the sea.

I know it was that sharp edge of solitude
That shaped and misshaped me.
What is good and what is bad, it shaped.
Yet it left me with a gift I could give myself.

I learned that I could escape, by letting the loneliness
fill me; letting the longing become so acute,

the need so desperate, that I could leave
myself and be with those who were not with me.

And so, my love, in the silence, in the solitude,
In the distance, I feel you, like one particle
Feels the other's spin. And I feel you now
So distant, that I too, am distanced from you,
And wonder if it is my love that has faded,
Or yours in the face of another.

The Pigeons of Zhulebino

Those first days in Moscow,
They were the enemy:
Their gray down gathering in corners
Like the frail remains of long dead cicadas.
Their droppings scarring the glass,
Melding with black soot.

On a flame of indignation,
Upon the sturdy stove of my ego
I boiled water to wash away
Their insults; as if, as if
They knew me and so
I had some right to tip their balance.

In the mornings I learn their control:
How easily they could penetrate my parallel world;
Interrupt those musky dreams that come
I the first moments of dawn.

I remember the satisfaction when I found it;
The long metal pole hidden in a corner.
I placed in beneath my bed,
That spear for my enemies,
When they came, disguised
As the sound of raining rice,
I raised the pole and beat beneath their claws.
So satisfying were the sounds:
Of metal striking metal,
Like bullets crackling in the cold air.
Their wings as fear lifted them away,
Their small sounds of shock.
I imagined myself a great warrior.

In winter the snow saved my sleep,
But when I awoke and sat drinking my coffee,
I watched them through the kitchen window,
Came to understand how well made they were.
Against the gray tongue of the Russian sky,
The colorless high-rises, everything tinted
By a smoky wash, they were only slightly darker
Gray gloves moving through the mysterious air,
Touching the world
Whenever and wherever they pleased.

In the midst of a storm, I noticed them
Clinging to power lines; whirling like tenacious
Rags in the wind.
I felt a small child's arm soft around my neck
How hard the wind was, and they,
needing mercy.

In the spring they began their cooing
Waking me even earlier then.
No longer needing the pole; the sound of bullets,
I toss small bits of bread at them
Wondering where they will lay their eggs.

<u>Conversations with Gertrude II</u>

"Were her buttons tender,
Were her nipples culled?"
Gertrude to me near
The shock of St. Michael's,

"Sometime in darkness,
perhaps once when she broke
along her finer lies"
I answer.

Gertrude's clean
and green into my blue
"No, but, just, but
Like a mournful mystery? Was she
bourbon before the mix?"

"It's not as it seems, Gertie,
Not as it seems. Her teeth
behold stereotypes, her tongue
Has never tasted a whisper,
She is brined and burns."

"When she swells,

the waves never crash."

As she does, Gertrude goes "Ohhh",
And then another long and
drawn out "Oooooohhhhh",
No my, just itself. "Well, you
know it is one thing to see a fine thing
strangely, quite another,
to mistake a strange thing for fine."
Off she goes into the finite night.

Trinity: The History of Three Orgasms

The cold is so deep in Vilnius
that my fingers, covered first in
stretched leather and then in down,
and curled into fists deep in my pockets
still sting and burn from the frost.

I.

The journey has been so long,
and I, so old and weary of it,
want only something soft to
rest my head on, and sleep.

But sleep does not come
and I am surprised to find
that I am vibrating with a desire,
that will not allow me anything
but its satisfaction.

As I press against my fingers.
I discover that I am, without reason, turbid.
I begin to move in a circle around it.
as the skin slides beneath my fingers
against its pliant firmness, I am so exquisitely
sensitive that it borders on pain.
I have gone too long, and I feel it now,
the ache of desire.

With these same fingers I moved inside you,
glided across your smooth slopes,
down into your flawless valleys; how
very, very focused I was then and I
wanted to force you open, to reach
deep enough to let my fingers
feather your cervix, and then
to make a fist.

I will not lie; I wanted your pain.
I wanted to stretch you, to test
the limits of what you could bear,
so that in the morning, when I was gone,
you would feel yourself bruised and sore
and remember me.

But it was too much, and
you wanted it over, and I
let you have your way...
although it was not what I wanted;
too quick and too soon
I let you go easy.

I feel the exquisite sensitivity
just before I start to come,
and I moan with it, but I have
denied myself for too long,
and the pleasure turns into
a sharp ache, like a pinch,
and the orgasm is unfulfilling, incomplete.

II.

"I have a surprise for you." she says
before she enters the kitchen. I am
cooking and she leans against me so
I can feel its solidity, running
from my coccyx, to the small of her.
I turn to look at it, and she takes my
hand to press against it. "For you, Mamita."
Simply that. She unbuttons her waist,
unzips her fly, and lets her pants fall.
Each vein bulges, protrudes, and its
head brushes against the inside of her
thigh. She holds the cock to the side,
takes my hand, and brings it between
her legs, and I feel her scrotum. I cup
the balls in my hand, and I am turned
on. I make them move between my fingers,
and carefully, so that I do not violate
any rules, I move in back of them, and
feel her wetness, take it up onto my fingers,
over and over again until her scrotum is
covered with her crystal-clear fluid, and

then I get down on my knees and lick.
I grind the balls, the belt against her clit,
As I suck her cock, her hands are soft in my
hair, and her words, so soft in my ears.

She takes me by the hand into the bedroom,
takes off my pants and nothing else, and lays
me on the edge of the bed. I look at the cock,
and feel the inkling of fear. "It is too much."
She smiles, "You are a woman, you are made
to stretch for big cocks and babies."

Everything is fine until the shaft enters and then,
I feel the burn, and then the pinch, and then the
pain. She does it slowly, so it is bearable, and I
do not, would never protest; she knows this. It
is always whatever she wants.

She begins to thrust and I turn my head
to bite the pillow, the pain is almost unbearable
now as she rises to the peak of her desire. I feel
the cock battering against me, I feel my womb
move with each thrust, and then she comes and
I am relieved.

But she will not be satisfied until I come, her
fantasy is not quite complete. "Tonight is the
night I will make you pregnant she says." She
begins again, slowly now, carefully, but all I
want is for it to be over. I force myself to
move against her, to moan, and then to pretend
that I am coming. "Take it out now." I say to her,

and when it comes out it is covered in blood.

My fingers catch the wave of the second orgasm,
they move down to my opening at the right second,
and I come hard, feel my insides throb, and I moan
and sigh, and turn my head to rest, but there is more.
It is not done yet.

III.

I imagine you as you were that night,
sitting on my back, and I submissive
beneath you. I imagine what I have
always imagined with you, with her;
as I lay on my side to put the condom
on your cock; as you reach for the lubricant,
as you put it at my entrance, and then
that moment of fear and anticipation,
as I feel its head laying loose against
my sphincter, as you ready yourself
to enter me, as I turn my head to bite
the pillow so I do not scream. I cannot
imagine the force with which you will
take me, but I know the feeling...the
head of the cock moving against my
cervix, pressing and punishing, the feel
of it stroking my uterus from without.
I know my orgasm with be long and slow
like water running softly from a hose
And when you are finished. When you are
done with me, the feel of your cock
inside me, and the small trickles

of blood blending with the melted
lubricant dripping from me.

The orgasm seizes me; and I feel
myself emptying into it, and then
as I lay there, the throbbing,
at the entrance to my rectum.
And I know at last I can sleep.

<u>I Am</u>

Deaf without the sound of your voice,
Your crying is muted to me, your sorrow
Hidden like a fallen woman's shame.

The smell of you is vanquished by time,
The taste of you taboo.
My arms hold nothing if they do not
Hold you. My fingers are without wisdom.

I have only my words, which are
After all, written on a machine,
Against an impure, imperfect white.
They have no melody; exist only as
The syncopated clicking of keys.
With the press of a button,
They are cast out into
The static resonance
That is the backdrop of the universe.

Soon I become vacuous,

Spinning without a vortex.

<u>Unknown</u>

How much we must hate those who love us
How much you must hate those who love you.
For the opposite of love is not hate, but indifference
Hate just the flip of the disc, of and for the record.

When you sit, turning their pictures like
Pictures, saying "Ohhh, and look....'
It is such a fine collection,
I think.

And then to gather them together,
Fleshy and firm, to set them before
You like living dolls, and pit them
Like pit bulls, pulling at each other's
Hair, the growl in the throat, deep
Not crisp, but rolling, like lottery balls.
When they come too close they are punished,
How much a matter of degree,
But it is the submission that perplexes me,
Not only must they suffer but they must be
Obedient, and obey their tormentor, so that
they can suffer more:
Turn your fingers
This way so I can pull the nails more easily;
Come to the room at this time on this day,
and I will excise your pain.

<u>Two Years Later</u>

Waking, I avoid the framed faces
Of your lovers past and present
By imagining the branches outside
Your glass and concrete
Are tributaries running through pure titanium?
Joining and conjoining, they flow until
Their identities are given up
To the rough and solitary river
They at last become.

Just as the sparrows are not ashamed
To shiver in the cold,
I am not ashamed to sleep alone.
After all, the cold does not belong to them,
And you do not belong to me.
We were not born into one another's lives
Neither will we die in one another's arms
Like those ancient lovers, their flesh eaten
By the centuries, yet
Bone still embracing bone.

What shames me is the precision of your lips
The experienced finger that poses my head.
How when my heart turns to leather,
You know how to make it supple,
Or when I am distant, the ease with which
You warm me into your embrace.

II.

In your arms
In your kitchen, in spring
You oh so casually mention
Your other lover
Ask me for what you have asked them for
"I love each of you differently, that is all."

My mind leaves you then on
Sightless, soundless wings.
The agony of an electric blue fish,
With a tail that falls like ribbons of silk,
Dying from the sudden shock of frigid water
Comes to mind then. I feel my muscles contract
To the point of pain, and I lose the ability to inhale.

<u>On the Porch</u>

Do you remember that morning I found you on the porch
Wearing a used mask?
Did you think you could hide yourself
Behind a countenance of porcelain?
Or that your colors did not blur
Into my consciousness.
That even with your mask I did not see you
Or that If I saw you,
I would love you less, or could not
Love you more.
As if it mattered that you were not a morning glory,
Or I your passing bloom?

<u>When I Envisioned You</u>

Sometimes when my vision encompassed you,
My love would not leave my body,
I fled your bed early then,
For to stay too long would only have
Made me beg not to leave at all.
The rules of the game would have been broken
And my staying would have frightened us both.

<u>Two Women in the Woods</u>

Why did he fall out of love with color?
What inner sorrow created this meditation in brown:
Rust, sienna and sepia, buff and taupe resting at their feet,
The only argument against it, the long strokes of drab green.

It leaves me wanting color: the red of your hair, the
Blue of my eyes, the titanium white
Stroked in the small of your back,
The paler rose of my nipples,
Your golden eyes,
Mixed on the canvas of a bed.

The women, faceless and dull, are yet strong.
The one in the forefront, with the strength to carry
The white burden of life in her arms, is like you.
And I am the other further down the path
Blurred and confusing, neither woman nor tree,
Yet both. But I have my strength too-
Which is pure stubbornness.

Oh, but how rigid they are, like the trees, immovable,
Roots deep in the ground, they rise up from it,
Straight and straight and straight,
While we are divergences and deviations,
that curve and entwine. Our portrait
Bending towards pastels.

<u>Tai Chi</u>

All you give me of earth's time,
Of your life, of your life in mine,
Are hours so precisely measured,
On tithed and tender days so treasured

They are held in mind as tethered horses.
Breaching mists, bracing in snows,
Or lathered, soaped in sun,
Scenting even in shade.
But carefully kept, well remembered,

The memories of your somnambulant arrivals
Calling on us to breath and breath and bow,
And with our hands to roll the energized ether;
To separate heaven from earth.
How we bent close to cobblestones
Only to rise like cobras
Coming into their balance -
Stretching our backbones long
Tilting our heads back,
Our gazes fixed.

You armed us and we became warriors.

With our fans we churned the sun
With our fists we pounded shade,
Our Bo Poles stirred the air
Spun the snow, bruised the rain
Chased the wind east again.

And oh, our invisible arrows,
How straight how fine their flight,
And our swords
How they glinted in moonlight
How they shined in the day,
As we plunged them into unknowns
One by one.
And all the while
The trees applauded.

And you, beautiful to your marrow,
Your outstretched arms balancing the day,

In the winter I see your breath billow,
Your foot slip against the ice,
And one finger, just one,
Just once, just hard enough,
Slide into the north wind.

I watch your back as you walk away,
Waiting to see if you will turn around.
Always in the distance always a red gate always slams shut.

And I move on
Aware of the improper conclusion.

<u>Nice</u>

My stomatologist hands them to me.
Pointing to the word written in Cyrillic on the box, he laughs.
"It says Nice because it is a very nice painkiller."
At home I take one then wait for Morpheus,
(Son of Hypnos, himself the son of Night and the twin brother of Death.
Sleep the short death, Death the long sleep)
To come to me, satisfy that desire that subsumes all others:
The end of Desire.

The pain leaves taking me with it
To a netherworld with its own dry river
Upon which I float suspended
Between sleep and wakefulness,
Without dreams or nightmares,
Simply drifting between alternative,
Callildascoping truths.

I surface to the sound of rain
On metal eves, on vinyl sills.
Listening, I come to understand
That its Essence resides
Neither in its sound or rhythm,
But in its weight, and with that
I understand that I have arrived at
A perfect knowledge of rain,
And the knowing is pure revelation.
And the weight of them, the rain, and the revelation,

Push me back into the weightless river.

Because the truth of you is untradeable
From my tablet, you appear to me
As the struggle for breath: a yellow apple
Filling a mouth, held in place by cyanotic lips
In the Black, in the drugged night, I lie,
Listening to the heavy stones of your tears.
Under their weight, I sink into the waterless river.

From other side of the kitchen, I watch
my toothless grandmother
struggling to chew an apple crescent.
Pity inflates me.
I wind myself around her legs
Place my head in her lap
where the woman truth of her is rising there.
Because she is a soft rock.
I climb her to her ears,
To chant "I love you; I love you."
Consumed with her struggle
To subsist, she ignores me.
No longer a virgin to indifference,
I acquire carnal knowledge of loneliness.
In the Nyx from which all things arise and pass,
I come to a precise understanding
Of the why and how of my love.
And the weight of it pulls me down again
into the dry dusty river.

It comes at me, buzzing with rage, fierce,
As if angry at me for being human.

I lift my blanket to cover my head
And in so doing, capture it close to my belly.
I lie there worrying that it will lay its larvae inside me.
In those dead and dying; I fear
That I will be eaten from inside out, disappear.
With that I comprehend the purity of Fear,
That basic rock under which we all sink,
Drying into dust.

I arise to the buzzing of the fly once again,
But no, it is not the buzzing of a fly,
There has never been a buzzing fly,
But only the flowing of my breath
Through my nose and throat,
I drifted on dust towards myself,
Towards you dreamed within me.

Longing

In the white of morning
In the sound of a single bird singing,
In the last hours of winter's wanting,
In a volume of incompressibility,
I stumble across our beginning.

Your stroke, defiant against its lines,
Crumbles me inward
Your echo against my ribs:
"Write me, send me you're writing."

And I write you from Orlando

And you write me from New York
"I will be on TV today"
And I watch you,
Spinning the miracles of your image
Across softly watered St. Augustine grass.

And I write you from New Jersey,
And you answer me from Pennsylvania.

Oh so briefly, we meet.
You make me wait too long
For mediated moments
Sprinkled with self-consciousness.
Head bending towards one another
I struggle to melt your distrust
Before the heat of my transparency

And I write you from Vermont
And you answer me from the Hamptons

In the summer of my discontent
Your words appear infrequently.
Abbreviated skeletons
Without flesh or feeling
Making mine come in torrents,
As I try to wash the fear from my marrow.

Alone in the norther woods,
Without the possibility of contact
I steal small stones from the shore
Worrying them with wistful gingers.

I wonder if I am lost.

And I write you from Provincetown
And you answer me from the city

I feel you now
A tornado moving in me
Churning poetry.
My words have blood in them
They throb and pulse.

And you write me from Switzerland
And I answer you from home.

Over time, I feel your distrust melting
Beneath my intensity.
I am not afraid of your absences
And you are not afraid of my closeness.

And I write you from my daughter's
And you answer me from your mother's.

Finally, on the streets of New York
We meet once again,
And I am no longer afraid of you
And you are no longer afraid of me.
And we kiss at long last.

<u>Seidy</u>

It is the next time now,
And as if time were an outsider, she comes to me,
Her hands full of pain and problems.
I know how it goes: her quick eyes
Will take my measure
As she notices every nuance,
Her perception is amazing, but nothing more.
She will far too casually ask her questions
Neither of us will acknowledge that
She is not asking what she is asking,
And that I have not answered her
With what she does not want to hear.

She searches the crevices of my kindness
For balm.
Without shame, she will reach for my heart,
Before turning to the kitchen.

She eats and eats and is still hungry.
I watch her mouth, thinking how I used to fill it
With myself,
Now it is filled with mint ice cream,
Then some guacamole,
She longs for cilantro to make it perfect.
She will take the meat sauce I have made
And turn it into a soup
Flavored with irritation.
Looking for more,
She will taste the cake and complain that it is too sweet
Before she cuts herself another piece.

She asks me over and over again
If I am hungry, and I shake my head
Remembering when I was so
Hungry for her.

Dissatisfied, she rises from the chair.
It will sigh as clearly as a woman
Finishing with her orgasm.
Before the door closes
I will begin to clear the dishes
She has left behind.

Remembrances

The smell of you upon my jacket,
Begins to dissipate.
Afraid that I would disappear forever,
I seal it in a plastic sleeve, never to be worn again.

The dried cheese and the salted fish we bought
That night near Lubyanka, were still in my refrigerator,
The sweet pieces of things:
The chocolate and the thin apple cookies.
The little loaves of French brie
Wrapped in a napkin from your hotel.
All of them put into them put into the freezer,
Not things, but memories frozen in time.

I found the large black bag I had taken from you
One the hall chair and tucked it away
Like a treasure.

What I could not save was the pain of you
Your hard suckle that arched my neck.
Just a dull ache now, it will soon leave me entirely
And our bodies will have separated at last.

On the Day She Left Paris

All the leaving, the having left,
Turned me as cold and clear
As December turns the Moscow River.
I would not cry for her when she left.
But Paris cried for her:
At first the tears came slowly spaced,
Later, saved for the shine on the stone streets.
At the Louvre, the long line of umbrellas waited,
And a chill bowed the head of the patient.
I, impatient, intolerant, cold, turn away from them,
Boarded a bus destiny placed before me.
Lived out the great freedom of those
Who belong to no one and to nowhere.

When the city's sorrow plays on its roof,
I moved on into the realm of the unfamiliar,
And there, a turn near the Madeline Church,
And another, before, as if on purpose
We pass you hotel.

The shock of the river cracking beneath my feet
Drew air from me, and there was nothing to replace it,
In the great, churning, emptiness
Where not feeling, no thought could reach out to save me.
The ice melted, and I felt myself drowning without her

Correction to the Present Perfect

He has the look of an English school boy.
His cream hair, not cut close like other Russian boys,
Crashed against his brow as he bows over his grammar.

I temper my voice, take a tint of reprimand on my brush
To mix with kindness and correct him on the present perfect.
In the narrow of his eyes
I see that he does not understand,
"I have loved hers for a long time."
From an indefinite period in the past to the present.

I see in his Siberian eyes a moment of confusion
As he senses but will not full grasp for a long time.
The inappropriateness, the heresy I have spoken to him.

"Do you understand?"
He nods his English boy head
And we resume.

The Wine of Curiosity

The wine has the vague taste of smoke
And when I lift back my tongue,
It releases the flavor of the wind.
Wound softly around ruby orbs
Their inside heated by the sun
Until they could bear it no more
And wanted only the relief of night.

Before the fireplace, my eyes upon you.
I lift the glass again.
And find layered upon the wind
My own longing and need
As I lifted the back of my tongue,
The swell of curiosity is overwhelming.

<u>Disconsolate</u>

It is the beginning,

we are sitting in semi darkness, drinking
I am a single myopic eye trying to focus:

(here the poet struggles
for the proper article: is it to be
"a," one of many different members
of the same class? Or "the,"
not the specific but the superlative.
She chooses the possessive).

Speaking of your long time lover,
you say of her, posited as a question:

"Do you know why I love her so much?"
My ears are funnels.
"Because she is so kind to me."
I am a cloth waiting for water.

"Do you know what she said?"

I am spoon with nothing to spin.
"I told her all I wanted to do
was watch tennis and do drugs."
I am an epitaph for no one.
"And she said, 'Well we can work that out.'"
I am a mute moth filling on wool.

"For my birthday, she gave me a picture,
of my ex-lover naked."
I am the kitchen table with nothing on it.
"She's really so kind isn't she?"
I am a blind woman,
fingering your question mark.

Icarus's Daughter (For E.)

Oh, Icarus, how your story has been twisted
To fit the need of myth.
It was never a king who held you captive
But The Queen of your demeaning,
And you were more that Dedalus's boy.
You were already a man

The father of your own driven dynasty.
Neither did you fly too high nor did you want to.
And it was not your wings that melted
But your heart that swelled beyond your body's bearing
And you never flew but ran from your prison,
And it was not the sun that enticed you.
But a kinder woman.

Oh Icarus, she took your sons
And made them hers.
As if possession were not enough.
She suckled them on her imperfections,
And wrapped them in the filament of her need,
And every day she added mor wax to their wings
And beautiful scarlet feathers
Plucked from a suffering bird.
And if your Greek Aristocrats
Thought they knew Arete
It was because they did not know her,
That excellent mother, those perfect children.
What more?

Oh Icarus, when she pointed them at the Sun
And told them to fly,
But the wings of the oldest were a heavy burden
one his back
Unable to fly, he did not try
But merely jumped to earth.
And the other new better than to try,
so, taking what succor he could
He fell asleep to die.

Oh, Icarus, it was your daughter, a woman
Born with the greatest imperfection
Who needed the most work?
For her, she allowed no false wings of wax.
Right after birth she separated her clavicles
From their tiny chambers,
And threw the years, drew them out
Further and further,

Until they were sharp and clear.
Then she bound them to the back of her arms
Until the flesh grew and covered them.
She would make her legs long,
Her fingers delicate to the piano,
She kept her ribs narrow,
And her nails, bright and sharp.
With her magic she turned her daughter
Into an eagle.

When the child cried, she chanted
"Lighter, lighter, you must become lighter"
The higher you will fly.
When the time came to push her from her perch,
She said, "Now fly to the sun."

Oh Icarus, how she flew on those painful wings,
And when she reached the sun, how bright she was.
But what she never let's be seen
Is the seared skin,
The place where the sun has bitten into her flesh.
Because perfection does not show its wounds.
Daily, she drinks her suffering,
Eats nothing but her pain.
As she circles the sun,
Obeying her the queen's wish.

Oh Icarus, do you understand now
Why they made you a disobedient boy with wax wings,
When you were really a man with a terrible destiny.
It was your daughter who, obeying the queens wishes,
flew obediently to the sun,

And your sons who died rather than try.
It was you who fled when he could,
And left your daughter to pay the price.

<u>Open Window</u>

It required an exceptional conspiracy of forces,
An exceptional alignment of events
(Tires disguised as the inaudible hum
Of waves crashing on a sponge shore,
The coordinated quieting of birds,
People, unrisen from their beds,
Holding their lives in abeyance,
My own pensive motionlessness.)
To give rise to the exceptional silence needed
For its abominable suffering to be heard.

A shuttle bucking on wanton heat,
Gathering up its energy, riding forward,
Returning, turning to charge again,
Its longing iterating and iterating,
Its frenzy a rhythm beaten out
with its own body.

I Imagine the stunning shock each time
It slams itself against the glass,
The painful jolt it endures before
It recedes and throws itself again;
This fine, frail Sisyphus, this determined
Slice of yearning and yearning life.

The nature of glass is incomprehensible to it.

A few feet away, a window is open.
All it need do to end its agony,
To free itself from its prison,
Is move on.
But it stays instead where it is,
Hurling itself against the impassible thing
That in its weakness it cannot shatter,
In its fixation it cannot escape.

In the end it will exhaust itself:
Its wings will pass to dust,
Its suffering rise to the Idea of Suffering itself.

It is Blake who formulates my question:
What exactly is the difference
Between the fly and I?

I, with my human mind,
Comprehend fully the nature of glass:
How it can be seen but not passed through;
How it comes to be and what it would take to be shattered.
I know the difference between an open window
And a closed one. Ignorance is not my excuse.
Yet I throw myself relentlessly against your panes;
Hit hard the hard barrier of your limits,
Feel the shock, withstand the pain every time;
Yet never move towards the wide-open window
But, consciously, deliberately away.

<u>Muse</u>

If there is any beauty in my words
It is your beauty filtered through my light

If there is any truth,
You are the wind on which it rises

When my words are gentle
Know that you are being drawn from my heart

And when my words are strong,
Know that you are the thunderstorm
That creates my lightening

When my words are subtle
You are their allusion

And when they are fierce
You are the air that feeds the fire

Should what I write touch anyone
It is only because you have touched me

For if I am the woman who writes
You are the woman for whom i write.

<u>For Katya</u>

Your eyes are the exotic mystery you have willed them to be,
To look into them directly is to gaze across spice markets,

From a distance, they are a breeze
Carrying the scent of sandalwood,

The distant memory of salty Asian lather
Roasting in the sun.

Your lips were formed in Russian forests,
Moistened by secret streams
That gave up the holy waters of Sergey Possad.
Before you were born generations of Russian women had painted them
On the sweet faces of carved wooden dolls,
Made to be hidden one inside the other,
Inside the other.

When you slipped into the world,
Those lips become actualized, become flesh.
Your voice was tuned to the sound of the streams,
And the smell of birch floated against your skin.
You were made to hide yourself inside yourself,
And then again, inside yourself, and then again.

It would be a year before I saw your smile.

Only your hands reveal you;
No unknowns can be cupped
Forever in your palms,
No secrets held long in your fists.
The past is written in them,
And the future waits for its oracle.

Your hands are wordless poems made to be read.

No truths can be hidden in our hands,
No unknowns kept cupped there.
Bold branches, your fingers reach out
For what you need, and in doing so
Unbind what you have bound.

For K: The Love Song of G.W.F. Hegel

Before being, before not being
Together began becoming,
When all was purest code,
And singularity – Gaia,
Nothing outside of her, all within.
Heavy and heated,
Waiting for her labor to begin.

Before there was front, before there was back,
When all was amorphous dust,
When from gravity's Attraction,
Yearnings pulled; spun out lust
Spinning out love.

Before breathing began, when breathing began,
When our antecedents crawled from the seas;
Before words waiting,
To be said
By mouths waiting to be created.

When stone shaped our consciousness,
When fire, then bronze, when iron,
When Mind was unravelling, exposing itself

As Self-Consciousness naming its categories,
Our names were waiting for us

II.

And we,

III.

For one another.
In the swarming here and now.
We walk through our rooms, come and go
Your sadness as true as the dry
Thin skin of my shame just so.
and I want you , and I want you to know.
The deep significance of the insignificant
Better put, nothing is insignificant,
But wet, saturated with worth;
Not least of all the breathing of a name.

VI.

And we,

VII:

My name is euphoria
Sparking in your eyes;
Yours, brave on my breath,
Silk unfolding on firm air.
Enveloping, proving presence, securing possession

Names and arms the same that way

IV.

And we,

V.

Last of all its writing.
Out of the well of night I draw my morning words,
Winding them, settling them on our loom,
Your rage no less than your joy finds lines,
Your distance and your closeness,
Your presence and your absence take positions
Squirming desires and dusty disappointments,
Valleys that rise and mountains that sink,
And oh god, oh god, your handsome beauty
Catching my breath.
All fated to be woven into a fine blanket
of metaphoric reductions written out in our names.

VI.

And we,

VII.

Must, cannot be, reduced to our names.
They are silver skin, slippery film;
Holding in place organs of hereness and nowness.
We breath no matter what we are called

By any other name we are stilled.

VII.

And we,

VIII.

Migrating birds, do not need to know the
Name of the destination towards which we fly;
Salmon, indifferent to what the difficult river is called;
Yet knowing well the when and where of arrival,
For what purpose to what end.
At the intersection of our entanglement ,
Nameless, fated, familiar, we said,
Under our breaths - "Oh, it is you."

IX.

And we,
Breathing purest coded air understand –
"All that is real is rational."
Everything is as it was meant to be.
Oedipus's hard lesson,
We cannot escape our destiny.

X.

And we.

<u>Slowing</u>

How still," she said, "the water is
Just before winter, late in the Fall.
The Moscow is thickening like an
Old woman's waist, and the Dnieper
Too."

Her face, a mirror flowing slowly.
Once turbulent, her bravery has become
A foiled eye; a minute glinting movement.
Rage and laughter wrapped in pale parchment;
A two-sided gift tied in single sided ribbons.

She rolls moments of time with her mind:
Great beauties and smaller victories;
Thinks of love as a memorable movie
Projected on the Manhattan skyline.
It had been her inheritance,
That impermanence and motion;
On its current she had floated always and everywhere.

Sometimes, and suddenly, she asks: "What was
The most beautiful place?" The variety is exhilarating
As she knows it will be. "Perhaps Petra" I say, "or the
Mexican beaches." The thin ribbons which hold her
Together threaten to unravel from pressured joy.

At night I watch her slow embrace and laying down
Of beloved disappointments; asking unanswerable
Questions before she turns to her right and becomes still.

With the drumming of her breath she enters
other dimensions, where her life is revised.

Before coffee she ponders her direction. Remembers lines
For her poem, observations of how thin the grass has become,
How frail before the onset of winter, and once again, how slow
And thick the Moscow River just before winter's freeze.
"Goa it will be for me this winter."
"Goa," I answer, knowing it will be the warm Nile instead.

<u>Fucking</u>

Let me tell you,
I have done enough of it
In my long life
To know what fucking is.

At seventeen I made a wise choice
And gave my virginity to a sweet boy
With blond hair, deep brown eyes,
And lips like James Dean's.
His cock was long and thin,
And if I had known what an orgasm was,
I would have had one.

Afterwards, I loved to fuck in the sea
On a moonless night, the waves moving the cock
The cock moving the water, in and out of me.

Because he was so handsome,
I married a man whose cock was
Too small and who knew no other way.
He gave me two daughters
Without satisfying me once.

I fucked a man whose cock
Was like a pencil, but whose
Tongue was a treasure. He began
At my toes and ended at my breasts
And everywhere in between was
Ecstasy.

My second husband was a little prick
Who would stay in me for hours,
His glazed eyes staring into mine,
His fingers tucked into my mouth.
It was years before he spoke his
Fantasy: how he was watching
A young woman getting gang raped,
And after that, I could not sleep with
Him again.

My first woman was a red head,
With wide blue eyes, who would
her come the second my fingers
Touched her, or or not come at all
It all depended, you see, on whether
She was going up or coming down
Off of her heroin high.

I used to fuck a neighbor who would

Come to my door in the afternoons,
While the children were at school.
She would ride my face until my jaw ached.
When she came, she would claw
The wall over the bed, shredding
The wallpaper I had chosen so carefully.

I fucked men and I fucked women,
And then I fucked a beautiful butch,
Who took me in every possible
Place, in every possible way, in
Every possible position. When I slept
With her I realized, I
Had never fucked before,

At the end of years of longing,
After years of wanting and needing,
You flew across oceans and continents,
And in London, at last,
I found myself laying in the same bed
With you.
But the shyness, the awkwardness,
The strangeness lay with us, and we played,
But we did not make love, did not come.

The next day, when I met you for dinner,
you asked me, as I expected, not to let
your lover know that we "fucked."
I laughed. I wanted to say to you,
but out of kindness did not:
"But my dear one, my love, we did not
fuck.

You see, I know what fucking is".